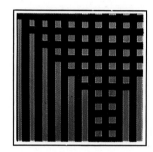

THE LIFE AND WORKS OF
RENNIE MACKINTOSH

Nathaniel Harris

SMITHMARK

Macintosh

This edition published in 1996 by SMITHMARK
Publishers, a division of U.S. Media Holdings, Inc.,
16 East 32nd Street, New York, NY 10016.
SMITHMARK books are available for bulk
purchase for sales promotion and premium use.
For details write or call the manager of special
sales, SMITHMARK Publishers, 16 East 32nd
Street, New York, NY 10016; (212) 532-6600
First published in Great Britain in 1996 by
Parragon Books Limited
Units 13-17, Avonbridge Industrial Estate
Atlantic Road, Avonmouth, Bristol BS11 9QD
United Kingdom

ISBN 0-7651-9897-5

Printed in Italy

Editors: Barbara Horn, Alex Stace, Alison Stace, Tucker Slingsby Ltd
                    and Jennifer Warner

Designers: Robert Mathias • Pedro Prá-Lopez, Kingfisher Design Services

Typesetting/DTP: Frances Prá-Lopez, Kingfisher Design Services

Picture Research: Kathy Lockley

The publishers would like to thank Joanna Hartleyat the Bridgeman Art Library
for her invaluable help.

CHARLES RENNIE MACKINTOSH 1868–1928

The career of Charles Rennie Mackintosh is marked by a series of painful paradoxes. During his lifetime he was famous in Vienna and Darmstadt; but he never received proper recognition in England or his native Scotland. He was an architect and interior designer of genius and a pioneer of the Modern Movement; yet he was virtually forgotten even before his death. More than almost any of his contemporaries, he was intent upon designing every aspect of a project, down to the light fittings and the cutlery; but his opportunities were tragically limited and his completed works were, more often than not, dispersed or destroyed. On the other hand, the once-forgotten Mackintosh has in recent years become such a cult figure that painstaking reconstructions of his work are now among Glasgow's most popular attractions.

Mackintosh was born in Glasgow on 7 June 1868. His father was a police superintendant, and he was the second of 11 children, but in some mysterious way he discovered his vocation as an architect. In 1889, having worked his way through a five-year apprenticeship, he joined the Glasgow practice of Honeyman and Keppie. From 1884 he was also a regular evening student at Glasgow School of Art, where he acquired important skills as a designer and watercolourist. At the school, Mackintosh, his friend Herbert MacNair and the sisters Margaret and Frances Macdonald became known as 'The Four', making a significant contribution to the flourishing 'Glasgow Style' of art nouveau, which had no counterpart in the rest of Britain.

In 1891 Mackintosh won a travelling scholarship which enabled him to spend several months in Italy. Back in Glasgow, however, he was still a subordinate at Honeyman and Keppie's, involved in a variety of more or less conventional commissions. Then in 1896 his designs won the competition for the new Glasgow School of Art. The first phase, completed between 1897–99, revealed Mackintosh's mastery as an architect and designer, although it received remarkably little publicity in Britain.

By contrast, the German-speaking avant-garde quickly responded when Mackintosh's work was featured in magazines. In 1900 Mackintosh and Margaret Macdonald, who had just married, were invited to contribute to the eighth Secession exhibition in Vienna. Mackintosh's white interiors and stylish furniture delighted Secession leaders such as Josef Hoffmann and Joseph Maria Olbrich, and he exercised an undoubted influence on the entire direction of Viennese arts and crafts. The Mackintoshes themselves attended the Secession exhibition and the 1902 Turin International Exhibition, which also showed their work to acclaim.

The situation in Britain was very different. The first decade of the 20th century was a busy period for Mackintosh. He designed and built the west wing of the Glasgow School of Art (1907-09), generally considered his masterpiece, as well as carrying out important domestic work and a series of remarkable tea room interiors on which he lavished talents that, arguably, might have been better used on major communal or private projects. But these were not forthcoming, and Mackintosh seems to have become increasingly embittered by lack of recognition. In 1904 he had become a partner in Honeyman and Keppie, but by 1913 he was drinking so much, and had become so unreliable, that the partnership was dissolved.

In 1914 the Mackintoshes left Glasgow, possibly intending to settle in Vienna, as their Austrian friends had been urging them to do. But while Mackintosh recuperated at Walberswick in Suffolk, the First World War broke out. In a country swept by spy mania, eccentric strangers were unwelcome in rural places and, since Vienna was out of the question, Charles and Margaret settled in the bohemian atmosphere of Chelsea in London.

The war made work hard to come by, and Mackintosh had only one significant commission, to remodel a house in Northampton. Although he had lost none of his skill, and seemed to be striking out in a new direction, none of his subsequent projects materialized. He and Margaret earned reasonable sums by designing fabrics, but in 1923 Mackintosh decided to give up the struggle and start a new career as a painter in watercolours. The Mackintoshes moved to the South of France, where Charles produced some fine paintings – which, inevitably, have never commanded the same kind of interest as his buildings and interiors.

In 1927 Mackintosh returned to England, where he was unsuccessfully treated for cancer of the tongue; a perfectionist to the last, he spent some time teaching the medical students how to make accurate drawings of his afflicted organ. He died in London on 11 December 1928, followed four years later by Margaret.

Detail

▷ **Orvieto Cathedral** 1891

Watercolour

IN 1889 CHARLES RENNIE MACKINTOSH finished his architectural apprenticeship and joined the practice of Honeyman and Keppie in his native Glasgow. While still a humble assistant, he won the prestigious Thomson Travel Scholarship, founded by the leading Scottish architect of an earlier generation, Alexander 'Greek' Thomson (1817-75). Mackintosh used the £60 prize to travel through the Continent to Italy, making sketches and taking notes. Living in Italy was cheap in those days, and the money lasted long enough for him to visit Venice, Florence, Rome and other art centres as far south as Sicily. Watercolour was always Mackintosh's favoured painting medium, although at this date he mainly used it as a way of recording what he had seen. The study of Orvieto Cathedral has a rather dutiful air, but it is significant that Mackintosh has chosen a close-up view that emphasizes the banded masonry; in this we surely catch an early glimpse of his taste for straight, severe lines.

◁ **The Harvest Moon** 1892

Watercolour

DURING THE EARLY 1890S, Mackintosh was engaged in relatively humdrum work as an assistant architect. Evening classes at Glasgow School of Art provided him with a more stimulating atmosphere, and painting became his most direct means of self-expression. *The Harvest Moon* is Mackintosh's earliest surviving art painting (as opposed to artistic record-sketches such as *Orvieto Cathedral*, see page 8). The style and subject matter are very much in the mystical-magical Symbolist vein of the 1890s. A young woman stands outlined against a brilliant moon, her hair and garments billowing out in a manner that became very familiar in art nouveau designs. The moon is circled by a feature like a Celtic torque (a twisted neck ornament) which culminates in a pair of wings framing the woman's head. But hidden in the cloud drifting across the moon is the outline of a naked woman – perhaps a Venus figure, set off against the chaste moon-goddess Diana. In the foreground, a tangled mass of spiky branches bars the way into this enchanted realm.

△ **Cabbages in the Orchard** 1894

Watercolour

IN THE EARLY 1890s Mackintosh formed close relationships with three other students at Glasgow School of Art, Herbert MacNair and the sisters Margaret and Frances Macdonald. The sisters in particular were working in an extreme Symbolist style, featuring elongated, skeletal figures, that caused them to be nicknamed 'the spooks'. Although his own productions were usually more restrained, Mackintosh evidently shared his fellow-students' interest in Symbolism, the Celtic Twilight, Rosicrucianism and other mystical currents of the period. As a group they became known as 'The Four', and exercised a remarkably strong influence, at first within the college and later more widely. Some of The Four's early works, including Mackintosh's *Cabbages in the Orchard*, appeared in an occasionally issued student album, *The Magazine*, with a strong literary and other-worldly tone. Mackintosh's watercolour, with its curious, balloon-like forms, is a cursory, evocative work, to which he added a jocular, highly oblique commentary.

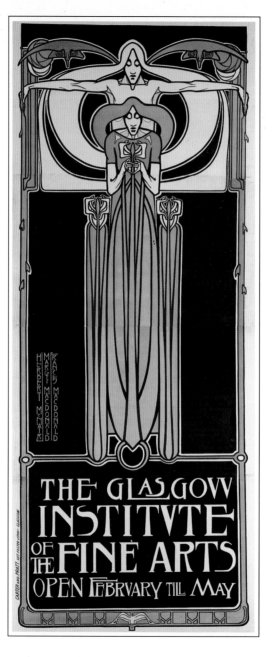

◁ **Glasgow Institute of Fine Arts** 1895

Poster

IN 1895-96 MACKINTOSH and other members of 'The Four' designed a number of posters, which entailed working in a much larger format than anything they had previously tackled. This early example is relatively conventional, with a robust, dominant female figure. However, Mackintosh's use of bold, flat colours was still unusual in Glasgow, although it had been pioneered in France by artists such as Toulouse-Lautrec, and taken up a year or two before by the Beggarstaff Brothers in London. Mackintosh's contribution is to simplify the design as much as possible, creating the woman out of a few lines and jigsaw-like areas of colour. He must have had happy memories of the Institute, which had awarded him many prizes when he was a precocious adolescent; and more recently he had exhibited *The Harvest Moon* (see page 10) there.

▷ **The Scottish Musical Review** 1896

Poster

EXECUTED A FEW MONTHS after the *Institute of Fine Arts* poster (see opposite), this is a much more daring design. The narrower format gives the poster a vertical emphasis in keeping with its hieratic, Japanese atmosphere. A stylized 'oriental' figure is posed in front of a disc, a favourite Mackintosh device during this period, seen in *The Harvest Moon* (see page 10) and the *Frieze* for *The Buchanan Street Tea Rooms* (see page 16). Mysteriously, a torque-like feature rises from a kind of grid that covers the face. Singing birds are perched on each side of the figure and merge with his/her costume. Mackintosh's design evidently owes a good deal to Japanese colour prints, but it is near-symmetrical and deliberately enigmatic. However, as later commentators pointed out, its bizarre appearance did mean that it fulfilled the essential requirement of a good poster, catching and holding the attention of the passer-by!

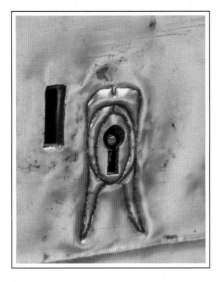

Detail

◁ **Jewel Box** c1896

Wood, brass and glass

LIKE SO MANY OF MACKINTOSH'S creations, this jewel box is remarkable in its modernity – which in this instance means the 'rough-hewn' look which only became widely fashionable several decades later. By contrast, the fleshy folds of the beaten brass plaque on the inside of the lid are typical of contemporary art nouveau forms, popular on the Continent, which Mackintosh generally avoided and is said to have disliked. The box was made for his sometime fiancée, Jessie Keppie. Jessie was the youngest sister of John Keppie, the junior partner in Honeyman and Keppie, the practice for which Mackintosh worked. From 1889 Mackintosh spent a good deal of time at the Keppies' country seat in Ayrshire, and by 1892 he was engaged to Jessie. Both belonged to a group of art students who jocularly called themselves 'The Immortals'.

Among them were the sisters Margaret and Frances Macdonald; at some point Mackintosh gravitated towards Margaret, whom he finally married in 1900. Jessie seems to have been devastated by the blow, and remained a spinster.

▷ **Frieze Design** 1896

Watercolour

THIS WAS A PREPARATORY DESIGN for the large frieze painted by Mackintosh on the walls of *The Buchanan Street Tea Rooms* in Glasgow. Mackintosh had shortly before met the owner of the tea rooms, Miss Kate Cranston, who became one of his most important patrons; her celebrated tea rooms in various parts of the city were like clubs, designed to attract Glaswegians not only for commercial reasons but also to keep them away from strong drink. The repeated female figure in the frieze is taken from an earlier watercolour by Mackintosh, *Part Seen, Imagined Part*, which he presented to his wife-to-be, Margaret Macdonald. At Buchanan Street, Mackintosh's role was a secondary one, in that most of the designs were the work of his fellow-architect George Walton; but the commission led on to Mackintosh's work at Argyle Street (see page 18), *The Willow Tea Rooms* in Sauchiehall Street (see pages 44-47), and at Ingham Street (see page 67).

Detail

▷ **Chair for The Argyle Street Tea Rooms** 1897

Oak

AT THE ARGYLE STREET TEA ROOMS, Mackintosh continued the partnership with George Walton which had begun at Buchanan Street (see page 16); but this time their roles were reversed, since Mackintosh designed most of the moveable items. The chair is an early example of a type for which he became well known, with straight lines and a high back; itself as striking as a work of sculpture, it also contributed to the distinctive appearance of Mackintosh interiors. The oval panel at the top gave the chair a throne-like appearance, recalling the 'haloes' for which Mackintosh had such a taste. The simplified bird shape, cut through the panel, was one of his happiest inventions. *The Argyle Street Chair* has been criticized as impractical – vulnerable and an impediment in a crowded tea room – but Miss Cranston evidently approved, and Mackintosh produced several variations on the same design.

▷ **Glasgow School of Art**
1897-99

GLASGOW SCHOOL OF ART WAS undoubtedly the finest of Mackintosh's architectural projects to have been built during his lifetime. In 1896, announcing the competition for the most suitable design, the governors of the school emphasized that the budget at their disposal was small, and that a very plain building was all that was required. Mackintosh's winning design took them at their word and, when it actually materialized, may well have disconcerted them. In an age when every respectable edifice boasted Greek columns or Gothic arches, the façade of the School of Art was revolutionary in its combination of huge windows and mostly plain masonry. The photograph shows the main (northern) façade on Renfrew Street; typically, Mackintosh created a deliberately asymmetrical design by placing the entrance off-centre.

▷ A Studio in Glasgow School of Art 1897-99

THE SIZE OF THE WINDOWS on the north façade can be appreciated from this photograph, in which students of painting can be seen working by the light that floods in through them; painters and sculptors normally prefer northern light, which is constant and even. The studios on the ground floor are 5m (16 ft) high, while those on the first floor reach a height of 8m (26 ft). Studios are the vital centres of an art school, and Mackintosh respected their workaday purpose by minimizing the amount of ornamental detail; his functionalist approach extended even to providing moveable partitions between the studios, so that they could be merged or their relative sizes adjusted. In view of Mackintosh's compulsion to design every item in an interior, and the original effects he achieved by doing so, his restraint here is deeply impressive.

Detail

◁ **The Mackintosh Room, Glasgow School of Art** 1897-99

THIS WAS ORIGINALLY THE board room, designed for meetings of the school's governors. It is possible that they never used it, since space was at a premium in the half-finished building, and the board room was soon converted into a studio. However, there are also indications that the governors did not much like this light, coolly beautiful setting, and the new board room designed for them by Mackintosh (see page 62) was certainly in a very different style. This interior, located in the east wing of the school, is lit from both east and west by large bay windows; and even when Mackintosh had to build a new fireproof staircase (see page 63) on the west side, he took care to preserve this distinctive feature. In 1947, in a belated act of recognition, this was renamed *The Mackintosh Room* and furnished with works by him that belonged to the school, including watercolours and objects such as light fittings from one of his most important domestic commissions, *Windyhill, Kilmacolm*.

◁ **Ironwork on The Glasgow School of Art** 1899

IN THE GLASGOW SCHOOL OF ART, Mackintosh anticipated 20th-century Modernism, turning away from the Victorian devotion to styles of the past and creating an essentially functional building. However, the school is also enlivened with many decorative details in Mackintosh's personal idiom. As always, he insisted on designing everything, including the wrought-iron railings, shown here in a detail of the main entrance. The oriental air of the ironwork is hardly accidental, and in fact the standard-like roundels rising above the railings (and each inhabited by a different small metal animal) were suggested by Japanese heraldic crests. The window brackets carry iron flowers on long stalks which are tied to the bars of the studio windows. The brackets were both fascinating and useful, serving to support the planks on which the window cleaners stood. The dramatically sculpted balcony and semi-circular window are also highly effective features, emphasizing the importance of the entrance area.

△ **The Director's Room, Glasgow School of Art** 1899

MACKINTOSH WAS EQUALLY innovative as an architect and as an interior designer – appropriately so, since he regarded the two roles as inseparable, aiming to make each building a complete, overall artistic statement. The director's room was among the earliest of Mackintosh's white rooms, which made a radical break with the dark tones of Victorian interiors and, in their spareness, with Victorian clutter. The walls are panelled, some of the panels actually concealing cupboards, and the cornice is as plain as possible but elegantly curving. Mackintosh's avoidance of symmetry is strikingly displayed in the way in which the windows are set in the bay. The large 'Willow Chair' belongs to a different place and period (see page 46), but most of the furniture was designed for use in the director's room.

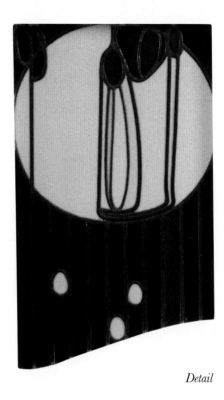

Detail

▷ **Bookcase** 1900

Oak and leaded glass

THIS MAGNIFICENT OBJECT seems to have been initially designed by Mackintosh for his own Glasgow flat at 120 Mains Street, early in 1900; later in the year he installed an almost identical bookcase (with a different leaded glass design) at Dunglass Castle, Bowling, as part of a programme of work there. The piece consists of identical cabinets flanking a magazine rack.

The severity of the white-painted oak is relieved by one of Mackintosh's most successful glass designs, poetic yet free from any suspicion of excess. The treatment suggests rather than presents images (flowers, a full moon, falling petals), and is evidently inspired by Japanese art without imitating it. Mouldings in the form of divided blossoms on long stems

(one of Mackintosh's hallmarks) add gentle curves of the most restrained art nouveau type, which prevent the straight lines and right-angles from making the design over-severe.

◁ **Cheval Mirror** 1900

Oak, glass and metal

THE FULL-LENGTH *Cheval Mirror* was once regarded as an indispensable item in any middle- or upper-class household, and Mackintosh designed a good many of them. Here his characteristic tendency towards elongation was justified functionally as well as making for elegance. This, the earliest to have survived, is a sturdy, stable object – but also an extraordinary, sculpturesque piece. It was shown at the Viennese Secession exhibition in 1900, and then kept by the Mackintoshes for their own use; it is now in the reconstructed Southpark 'house' in the Hunterian Museum, Glasgow (see pages 54-60). It is made of white-painted oak, with coloured glass panels and silvered metal handles. The little red glass buds, set on unobtrusive stalks, glow when they catch the light. The neat sets of drawers on each side served as useful repositories for cuff-links and similar items.

▷ **The Daily Record Building**
1901

Watercolour

In 1901 Mackintosh designed new offices in Renfield Lane for a well-known Glasgow newspaper, the *Daily Record*. The site was a difficult one, since the lane was very narrow, about 5.5 m (18 ft) across, with high buildings on either side. Consequently Mackintosh's fine design is impossible to view (or reproduce) adequately; and his watercolour is the only survivor of the original designs. The ground floor is faced with stone, with an undulating band along the top. The storeys above are faced with white ceramic tiles to offset the darkness of the lane. At the very top of the building, the dormer (roof) windows are set in red sandstone. Mackintosh's design illustrates brilliantly how an apparently plain modern façade can be simultaneously adapted to awkward circumstances and enlivened with a few discreet touches of detail.

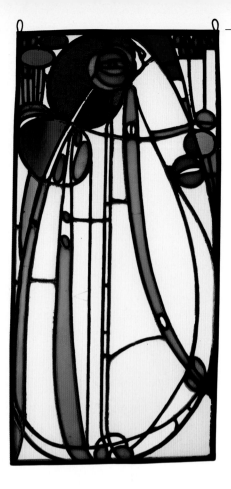

△ **Stained Glass Panel** 1902

AS A DESIGNER, MACKINTOSH made extensive use of glass in both translucent and reflective (mirror) form. The one church that he designed and built (Queen's Cross, Glasgow, 1898) was furnished with traditional stained glass windows, but elsewhere his stained and leaded glass was made for secular interiors, often in distinctive combination with mirror glass, as in

The Willow Tea Rooms (see pages 44-47). Mackintosh was habitually sparing in his use of strong colour, and some of his subtlest effects were obtained on furniture with very small inset pieces of glass which glowed – rather than blazed – when they caught the light. Even the stained glass panel shown here has an almost neutral background which serves to enhance the areas

that are coloured. The panel is a delightful example of a stylized floral composition which exists on the frontier between the organic and the geometrical. Mackintosh's affinities with the sinuosities of art nouveau are very apparent, but his restrained treatment prevents the work from falling into the 'decadent' lushness of the style.

▷ **Haus Eines Kunstfreundes** 1902

Lithograph

IN 1901 MACKINTOSH submitted designs for a competition sponsored by a German magazine, using the pseudonym *Der Vogel* (The Bird). The competition, to design a sumptuous *Haus Eines Kunstfreundes* (House for an Art Lover), spurred Mackintosh to create a princely private dwelling – something he never had the opportunity to carry out in reality. For technical reasons his entry was not eligible for a prize, but the judges praised it enthusiastically and gave it a special award. The designs were published in Germany the following year as a lithographic portfolio, for which Mackintosh created this frontispiece; its elongated art nouveau style is somewhat misleading, in that the actual building and its interiors were masterpieces of early Modernism, almost austere in their clean-cut geometry. Mackintosh received an impressive posthumous tribute from Glasgow in 1990, when the house was finally built to his designs in Bellahouston Park.

IDEEN-WETTBEWERB FUR EIN HERRSCHAFTLICHES WOHNHAUS EINES KUNST-FREUNDES

DAS SPEISE-ZIMMER.

14

CHARLES
RENNIE
MACINTOSH
1 9 1

GOW. HAUS EINES KUNST-FREUNDES
ANDER KOCH-DARMSTADT. · TAFEL XIV

◁ **Design for a Dining Room** 1902

Lithograph

THIS IS ONE OF THE DESIGNS published in Mackintosh's *Haus Eines Kunstfreundes* portfolio (see page 31). Unlike some of his successors in the Modern Movement, Mackintosh was aware of the need for variety in interiors of any great size. Consequently the reception room and music room of the art lover's house were shown as painted white, but the north-lit hall and dining room were dark and oak-lined; however, the pretty panel designs, curved white ceiling and general spaciousness made the scheme far from oppressive. Mackintosh's portfolio greatly increased his reputation in German-speaking countries, but may actually have harmed it in Britain. It would be an over-simplification to say that Mackintosh was admired abroad and entirely ignored at home … but perhaps only a true-British publication such as *Our Homes and How to Beautify Them* (1902) could have reproduced this lithograph while denouncing its subject without qualification as 'dreadful' and 'mad'.

▷ **Chair** 1902

Oak, upholstered

PAINTED WHITE, WITH a tall back carrying a stencilled design of roses, this chair is one of Mackintosh's most striking creations. A highly effective feature is the way the back tapers upwards, parting company with the uprights. Above all, the proportions are memorable, although their functional virtues are questionable. The chair is very tall, 152.5 cm (60 in), and arguably makes the most favourable impression when unoccupied. Nevertheless it did find a buyer. It was shown at the Turin International Exhibition in April 1902, where Mackintosh had a meeting with his Viennese patron, Fritz Wärndorfer, who had already commissioned Mackintosh to design a music salon for him. Warndorfer ordered several of the chairs for the salon; this one, however, was kept by Mackintosh and is one of the items in the Southpark Avenue house recreated in the Hunterian Museum, Glasgow.

▷ **Margaret Macdonald Mackintosh** (1864-1933)

Magazine cover 1902

MACKINTOSH'S WIFE, MARGARET MACDONALD, contributed panels and other designs to his interiors, as well as working as an artist in her own right. Mackintosh liked to claim that she had genius, whereas he himself had only talent; but few people have shared this view. In fact Margaret's fanciful art nouveau-Symbolist style can be seen as a weakening influence on Mackintosh's more rigorous Modernist approach. On the other hand, Margaret's faith and conviction does seem to have inspired Mackintosh and acted as a stabilizing influence during their hard times later in life. The periodical *Deutsche Kunst und Dekoration (German Art and Decoration)* was an enthusiastic advocate of Mackintosh's work from 1898, and its publisher, Alexander Koch, promoted the momentous *Haus Eines Kunstfreundes* competition (see page 31).

Künstlerische Kostüme ∗ Porzellane ∗ Fotogr. Porträts ∗ Buchgewerbe.

V. JAHRG. HEFT 8. MAI 1902. EINZELPREIS M. 2.⁵⁰

◁ **Oval Table** c1902

Wood and leaded glass

A STRIKINGLY ORIGINAL
CONCEPTION, this table has ten legs
– five at each end, tapering
upwards and flattened so that,
irrespective of the angle from
which they are seen, they appear to
have a pleasing variety of shapes
and sizes. Between each outer pair
of legs there is a little panel with a
characteristic bud-like design,
inlaid in leaded glass. The table, or
its duplicate, was part of the music
salon designed by Mackintosh in
1902 for Fritz Warndorfer, a
wealthy Viennese; celebrated in its
own day, the salon suffered the fate
of so much of Mackintosh's work,
disappearing virtually without
trace. By 1902-03 Mackintosh was
so well known on the Continent
that he was able to exhibit a room
at the World of Art exhibition in
Moscow, organized by Serge
Diaghilev (later famous as the
mastermind of the Ballets Russes).
Surviving photographs show this
table, or a replica, among the
exhibits.

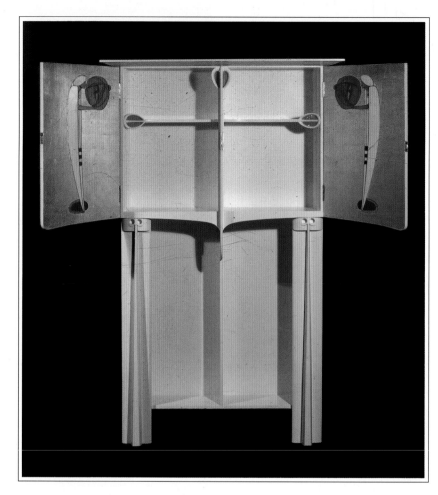

◁ **Cabinet** c1902

Oak, glass and metal

THIS CHINA CABINET WAS one of a pair designed by Mackintosh for a client at Kingsborough Gardens, Glasgow. It was evidently intended to remain open most of the time – to display the china, the restrained art nouveau curves of the woodwork, and above all the decorative insides of the doors. These are painted silver and inlaid with coloured glass; the familiar Mackintosh cabbage rose is associated with a stylized female figure very much in the manner of the designer's wife, Margaret Macdonald, and the contemporary Glasgow School. Mackintosh had a pair of these cabinets made for himself, with four metal hinges on each door rather than the two on the version shown here; these supported the door more effectively as well as improving the appearance of the cabinet when the doors were shut. Mackintosh's own cabinets stand in the reconstructed house in the Hunterian Art Gallery, Glasgow (see pages 54-60).

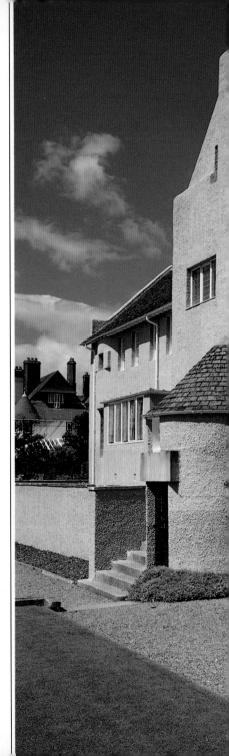

▷ **The Hill House, Helensburgh** 1902-04

AS AN ARCHITECT, MACKINTOSH received only two commissions for domestic buildings of any real significance. One was *Windyhill, Kilmacolm*, designed in 1899 and built by 1901 for the businessman William Donaldson. The other, *The Hill House*, was similar in plan but larger and more ambitious. It was built on a terraced site overlooking Helensburgh and with fine views of the River Clyde. The grey harled (rough-cast) walls harked back to traditional Scottish building practice although, unlike many of his contemporaries, Mackintosh never directly imitated past styles. The house is approached from the west, through wrought-iron gates designed by Mackintosh; on this side it is imposing, with a plain wall and a large chimney with one sloping ('battered') side. The south side is less formal, incorporating a distinctly Scottish feature, a round stair tower tucked into the angle made by two walls. The overall impression is of a building that is comfortable, modern, and very much in harmony with the landscape.

▷ **The Main Bedroom, The Hill House, Helensburgh** 1902-04

MACKINTOSH WAS ONE OF the pioneers of the use of white in interiors. He particularly favoured it for bedrooms, as is apparent here and in the design of his own house (see page 60). At *The Hill House* Mackintosh placed the main bedroom at the end of a corridor, maximizing the privacy of the owners. The room itself is L-shaped, dividing naturally into two parts. The bed and fitted wardrobes stand in a vaulted alcove. The other area, seen here, provides some living space, with a wash stand, a fine fireplace, and a bay running the length of the room; inserted into it are a fireside couch and two more wardrobes, decorated with stylized plant form mouldings and pink and green glass inlays. Other notable furnishings are the table, with its blade-like legs, and the equally striking, but less practical, ladderback chair.

▷ **Fish Knife and Fork** c1903

THE CONCEPT OF A 'TOTAL' work of art was fashionable during Mackintosh's heyday, but he was near-unique in his rigorous attempts to put it into practice. His works usually included a few decorative panels by his wife and close collaborator Margaret Macdonald, but except for these he preferred to design every element in a project, starting with the building itself. Although this proved to be possible on tragically few occasions, Mackintosh was more fortunate in his commissions for interiors. At *The Willow Tea Rooms* (see pages 44-47) his activities extended beyond the cutlery to the appearance of the waitresses' uniforms; and he is said to have slipped into the building before it opened in order to arrange the cut flowers in a suitable manner. The fish knife and fork by Mackintosh are superbly audacious in their disregard of traditional forms; the design of the knife is in fact perfectly logical, since a fish knife separates rather than cuts, and therefore hardly needs the customary long edge.

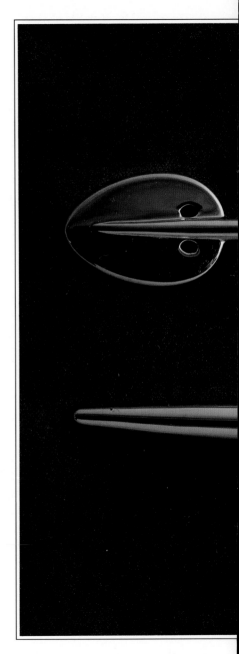

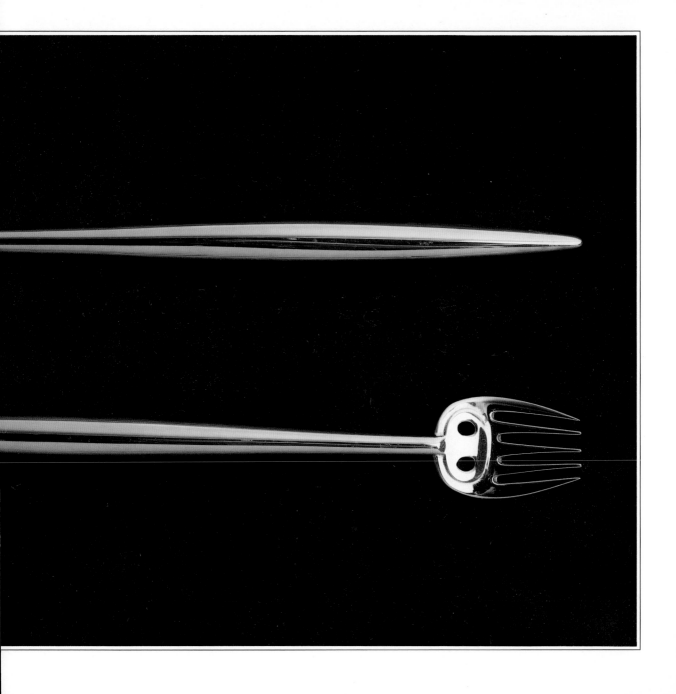

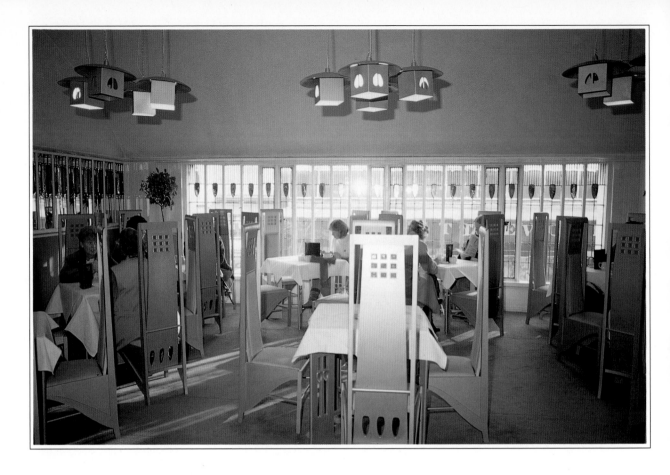

△ **Room de Luxe, The Willow Tea Rooms, Glasgow** 1903-04

Partial reconstruction

THE WILLOW TEA ROOMS was Kate Cranston's fourth establishment in Glasgow, opened in a terrace in Sauchiehall Street ('Willow Grove' Street in Gaelic). Since it was a new venture, Mackintosh was able to design the premises in every detail, right down to the cutlery; he even remodelled the façade into a cool modern frontage, separated by narrow chequered bands from the very different shop fronts on either side. The interior showed Mackintosh at his most opulent, especially in the first-floor *Room de Luxe*. This was entered by splendid double doors made of stained and leaded glass, and a series of stained and mirror-glass panels ran round three sides of the room (opposite), complementing the long, vertically divided windows on the fourth side overlooking Sauchiehall Street. Fortunately these features survived the ravages of time, and the *Room de Luxe* has been reconstructed and is back in business.

▷ Panels in The Willow Tea Rooms 1904

Stained glass and mirror glass

MACKINTOSH'S ORNAMENTAL DESIGNS for *The Willow Tea Rooms* were among his most spectacular works. These extraordinary panels in the *Room De Luxe* (see opposite) run around three sides of the room, their rich purple and patterns of rounded oblongs creating a lovely but somewhat strange effect, especially in association with a prominent gesso (plaster) panel by Margaret Macdonald in characteristic poetic vein. Now-vanished elements elsewhere in the building must have reinforced the impression that the Mackintoshes had created a kind of shrine, filled with a solemn symbolism that was a little incongruous in a tea room. Arguably this was a tragic result of Mackintosh's limited field of action, which meant that he was engaged in designing tea rooms at a time when, as a major architect, he should have been inundated with requests for great communal and private projects; but it is possible to hold the contrary opinion – that these unusual commissions are one of the things that make Mackintosh so interesting.

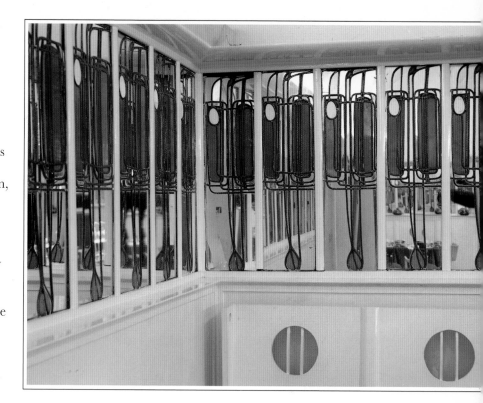

Detail

▷ **Order Desk Chair for The Willow Tea Rooms, Glasgow**
1904

Ebonized oak

MACKINTOSH MADE THIS roughly semicircular chair for the ground floor section of *The Willow Tea Rooms* (which, unlike the *Room de Luxe*, page 44, has not been restored). The 'Willow Chair' is one of his most accomplished pieces, maintaining the tree theme of the tea rooms through the lattice design on the back, which is outlined by the 'background' of vertical bars. One of the most stylish features is the way the top of the seat protrudes beyond the sides, its front then sloping back and down to rest a little inside them. The chair was placed in landmark fashion at the junction of two separate decorative schemes. It was for the use of the supervisor at the order desk, to whom the waitresses brought customers' orders; the supervisor was able to notify the kitchen below by code, dropping appropriately coloured balls down a tube.

Detail

▷ **Writing Desk** 1904

Ebonized oak, glass and mother of pearl

MACKINTOSH CREATED THE design of this desk for *The Hill House, Helensburgh* (see pages 38-41). The object actually shown in this photograph is a replica he had made for his own use at the Mackintoshes' Mains Street flat in Glasgow; it is now part of the reconstructed library-studio in the Hunterian Art Gallery (see pages 54-60). Here the doors are shown wide open; when they are shut, the piece gives a rather different, more compact and substantial, impression. It is certainly more solid and also more sumptuous than most of Mackintosh's previous furniture, for the first time incorporating mother of pearl ornament. An even more important decorative device was the marshalling of small open squares into geometric shapes, often arranged like lattices of various sizes; these would reappear often in Mackintosh's work (see pages 46, 50, and 67).

Detail

▷ **Writing Table** 1904

Oak and glass

BY 1903 MACKINTOSH HAD become Miss Kate Cranston's favourite designer, with commissions for three of her Glasgow tea rooms behind him. She then invited him to redecorate the interiors of her own dwelling, Hous'hill, at Nitshill, Glasgow. The work was done in 1903-04, and included a good deal of new furniture. The house was demolished in the 1930s and its furniture sold off at auction, but a handful of pieces have since come to light and have been more or less certainly identified with the help of old photographs of the interior. This writing table seems to have stood in the Blue Bedroom. The writing surface was a fall-front flap supported on gate legs, so that when the legs were swung inwards and the flap was raised, the table became a compact, unobtrusive object. When set out for use, the table displays a glass panel among the pigeonholes with an elegant Mackintosh rose design.

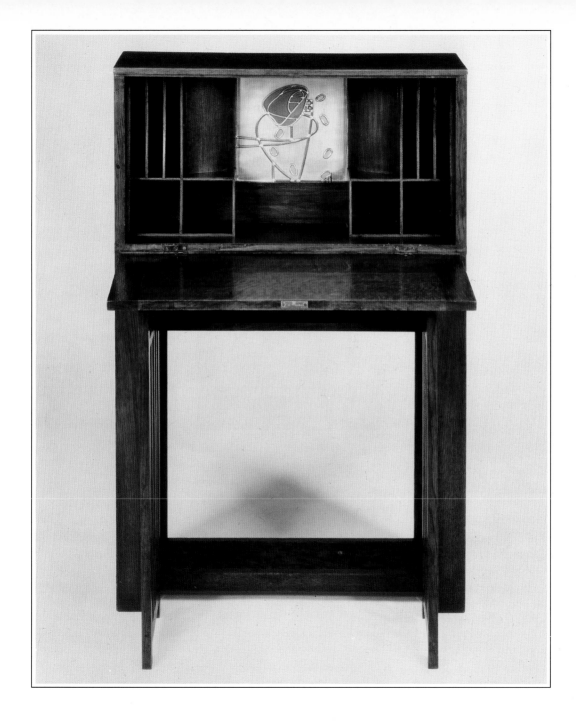

Detail

▷ **Scotland Street School, Glasgow** 1904-06

MACKINTOSH DESIGNED *Scotland Street School* in 1903, while *The Hill House* (see pages 38-41) was being built and finished. At this point, despite the controversial nature of his work, his career seemed promising, and in 1904 he became John Keppie's partner in the firm of Honeyman and Keppie (Honeyman, the senior partner, had retired). Scotland Street

School was a 'Board School', that is, a state school roughly equivalent to the modern primary school. Financial constraints and the need to adhere to a standard plan restricted Mackintosh's options, but he still managed to create an extensively glazed (and therefore light-filled) building with a certain distinction. In particular, the two cone-capped staircase

towers (actually the girls' and boys' entrances) pleasingly evoke the 'Scottish Baronial' tradition, while there is an ultra-modern look about the cloakroom areas, the upper storeys progressively receding to dramatize the adjacent towers. The building is now a museum of education.

Detail

▷ The Hall, Southpark Avenue, Glasgow

Reconstruction in the Hunterian Art Gallery, Glasgow

IN 1900 MACKINTOSH MARRIED Margaret Macdonald, and the couple settled in a flat at 120 Mains Street, Glasgow. The interior was remodelled by Mackintosh and furnished with items designed by him. In 1906 the Mackintoshes moved to a house in the Hillside area, 78 Southpark Avenue, which represented a distinct social step upwards. Again Mackintosh remodelled the interior, but most of the furniture came from the Mains Street flat. The Mackintoshes lived in Southpark Avenue until they left Glasgow in 1914. The house was later demolished, but the interior has been faithfully recreated, on the basis of records and old photographs, at Glasgow's Hunterian Art Gallery. This photograph and the three that follow (see pages 56-61) show some of the results. The Hall is elegant but relatively small and dark; Mackintosh rather liked to introduce his interiors unpretentiously, so that visitors remained unprepared for the celebration of light and space to come.

▷ The Drawing Room, Southpark Avenue

Reconstruction in the Hunterian Art Gallery, Glasgow

IT IS NOW DIFFICULT TO REALIZE just how radical an interior such as this one must have seemed in the early 1900s. The whiteness of the walls and furniture would have struck most of Mackintosh's contemporaries as unpleasantly icy, and the sparseness of the furniture as eccentric; at least one visitor did wonder whether the house was still only half furnished. In reality, the positioning of every object was premeditated. Many had been brought from the Mains Street flat, including the fireplace with its wonderfully elegant curves, the cabinets on either side of it (near-identical to the one on page 37), and the chair with a high stencilled back (see page 34). A traditional Scottish note – though an oddly assertive one – is struck by a low-seated, box-like lug chair, although the carved round plaques on the arms are in a more familiar Mackintosh style. Doubtless an important element of the decor was the pair of grey corduroy cushions, one on each side of the fireplace, reserved for the Mackintoshes' Persian cats.

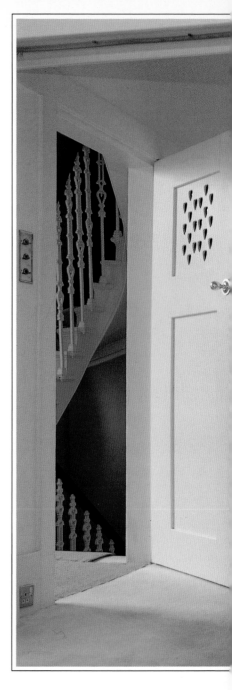

▷ The Studio-Library, Southpark Avenue

Reconstruction in the Hunterian Art Gallery, Glasgow

IN REMODELLING THE INTERIOR of the Southpark Avenue house, Mackintosh turned the first floor into a single, L-shaped, open-plan area. The amount of light was increased by inserting a window into the gable wall, while its quality was controlled and diffused by large muslin curtains. Curtains were also used, when needed, to partition the first floor into a drawing room (see page 56) and *The Studio-Library* shown here. This was notable for a striking contrast between the white setting and the mainly dark furniture, perhaps prompted by the unavoidable darkness of the covers of the books in the shelves on each side of the chimney breast. The two finest pieces of furniture, designed a few years before the Mackintoshes moved to Southpark Avenue, were the large white bookcase of 1900 (see page 26) and the imposing 1904 writing desk (see page 48).

▷ **The Bedroom, Southpark Avenue, Glasgow**

Reconstruction in the Hunterian Art Gallery, Glasgow

AS NOW RECONSTRUCTED, *The Bedroom* is the most thoroughgoing exercise in sheer whiteness in the Southpark Avenue house (perhaps whiter than it ever was in Mackintosh's day). As in the other rooms, many objects were not new, but were transferred from Mackintosh's previous home at 120 Mains Street. The ornamental details on the wardrobes, the *Cheval Mirror* (also shown on page 28) and the bed are among Mackintosh's most exquisite creations, vivified by little glass panels which catch the light and scatter points of colour. The bed is an elegant, modern variation on the classic four-poster, substituting clean lines and white paint for the traditional dark, massy oak. The silvered metal panel above the fireplace is by Margaret Macdonald Mackintosh.

△ The Board Room, Glasgow School of Art 1906

THIS REPRESENTS A re-modelling
by Mackintosh of a ground-floor
room in the School of Art;
structurally the room dates from
the 1897-99 phase of construction.
The first board room (see page 22)
was converted into a studio
because of lack of working space,
and perhaps too because the
governors felt that it was not

sufficiently dignified. At any rate,
Mackintosh's design for the new
board room was, by his standards,
an extremely conventional one,
with the dark, polished wood
panelling associated with solemn
councils and committees. Sections
of the panelling are separated by
pilasters, flattened column-like
elements that project slightly from

the wall. These are evidently
inspired by the classical Greek
Ionic order, with fluted (grooved)
trunk and prominent scrolls at the
top, but Mackintosh's treatment is
stylized and idiosyncratic, for
example reducing the scrolls to
little blocks. The furniture, also
designed by Mackintosh, is of
polished cypress.

▷ The East Staircase, Glasgow School of Art 1907

The School of Art's principal staircase is an impressive lofty work, built during the first phase of construction in 1897-99. Unfortunately it was also the only staircase, and the newly built school was in contravention of fire regulations. Although this was realized, the official opening of the school went ahead in December 1899, with buckets of sand and water in the corridors and, most embarrassing of all, the fire brigade in attendance. Nevertheless nothing more was done until the second phase of building began in 1907, when Mackintosh inserted two new fireproof staircases. He fitted this one neatly into an angle in the already built east wing, dividing the wall surface beside the stairs into a lower part in a dark, cement-rendered finish, and an upper part of exposed brick. An occasional square ceramic tile supplied a decorative note, but the general effect was rugged and sculpturesque; in the photograph this is enhanced by the wrought-iron grille.

▷ **West Façade, Glasgow School of Art** 1897-1909

The School of Art was built in two phases, of which the first was completed in 1899. After an interval of several years, Mackintosh was commissioned to design the west, or library, wing, and to add an attic storey to the entire building. Work on the project started in 1907. Mackintosh was now at the height of his powers, and the *West Façade* is much more audacious than anything he had attempted before. The difficult nature of the site – its steep slope – is turned into an advantage, making the building appear to soar, and the great vertical bays of glass and masonry draw the eye all the way up the façade to the solid gable. Curiously enough, while the designs for *The Glasgow School of Art* created a certain amount of local controversy, the completed building caused no great stir in Britain and did little or nothing to advance Mackintosh's reputation outside his native city.

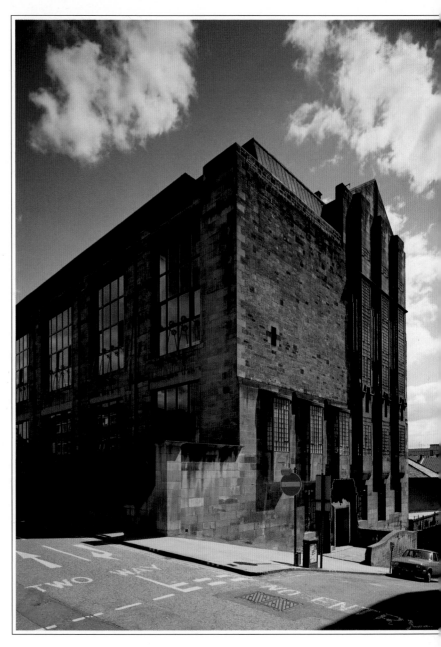

▷ **The Library, Glasgow School of Art** 1909

THE LIBRARY IS ONE OF
Mackintosh's masterworks,
stamped with his personal style
yet designed in a fashion entirely
appropriate to its intended use.
The rich brown woodwork creates
an atmosphere favourable to
study, accentuated by the severe
presence of plain timber pillars
rising from the floor. The
appearance of the pillars changes
at the level of the gallery, which is
linked to them but set back about
1m (3.3 ft) and supported on
beams; thanks to the modest
dimensions of the gallery, the
students below do not feel
hemmed in. The pillars continue
upwards to meet the coffered
ceiling, whose lattice form was
much used by Mackintosh (see
pages 46, 50 and 67). The space
between each pillar and the
gallery wall is filled with elegantly
twisted and coloured balusters.
The lampshades hanging in
clusters from the ceiling are
astonishingly modern in design,
directing the light downwards into
the study area. As usual, all the
furnishings were designed by
Mackintosh himself.

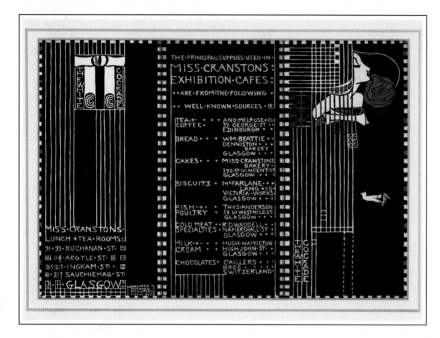

△ **Menu** 1911

▷ **The Chinese Room,
Ingram Street, Glasgow**
1911

UNTIL ABOUT 1911, Margaret Macdonald Mackintosh was involved in many of her husband's decorative schemes, contributing embroideries, gesso (plaster) panels, beaten metal plaques and similar items. Her menu card was designed for the White Cockade, a temporary tearooms set up at the Glasgow International Exhibition by Mackintosh; his client was, yet again, Miss Kate Cranston. Almost nothing is known about Mackintosh's scheme, which may well have resembled one of the rooms he redesigned at Ingram Street later in the year (see opposite). The white cockade was the badge adopted by Bonnie Prince Charlie and his followers during one of the most stirring episodes in Scottish history, the 1745 rebellion – in spite of which Margaret chose to feature the Mackintoshes own rose-symbol, along with familiar motifs such as the chequer pattern. Though still hinting at mysteries, the menu design is much bolder than most of Margaret's work.

THE INGRAM STREET TEA ROOMS was one of four establishments, owned by Miss Kate Cranston, for which Mackintosh provided designs. At Ingram Street the premises consisted of a number of interconnected rooms which were added to over the years; Mackintosh worked there in 1901 and again in 1907. In 1911 he received his most important commission, to redesign two rooms which became *The Cloister Room* and *The Chinese Room. The Chinese Room*, an exercise in oriental fantasy in the heart of Glasgow, is one of his most exotic achievements. The room is dominated by blue-painted lattice work, mostly in the form of screens, although a large latticed pay box also plays an important part in the scheme. Screens are used to lower the ceiling and, in combination with partitions, create an enclosed, mysterious effect. Chairs with fretwork rails emphasize the geometry of the setting, which would lead on to Mackintosh's art-deco-like work in the *Bedroom* at Derngate (see page 70).

Detail

▷ **Anemones** c1916

Pencil and watercolour

HAVING DISSOLVED HIS partnership with John Keppie and failed to establish his own independent practice, Mackintosh left Glasgow for good in 1914. He moved south, first to Walberswick in Suffolk and then to Chelsea in London, painting more often and more ambitiously than he had done for years. At Walberswick he produced a few landscapes and a larger number of delicate, spiky flower studies. *Anemones* is probably later, belonging to a group of larger and more finished paintings of cut flowers which Mackintosh hoped to publish as a book. The treatment of the flowers is extremely naturalistic, so that their organic quality contrasts sharply with several different forms of artifice – the striped cylindrical vase and the mirror, in which we can see the reflection of the bouquet in front of bookshelves and an elaborate, abstract textile design.

Detail

▷ **Bedroom** 1916

THE GUEST BEDROOM at 78 Derngate, Northampton, is one of Mackintosh's boldest designs, illustrating his development towards a geometric art-deco-like style. Mackintosh's brief was to remodel Derngate, a small red-brick Victorian house. Since it was part of a terrace, major changes were impossible, but Mackintosh's solutions were characteristically ingenious and elegant; his cool, rectilinear garden front was arguably the first example of Modernist architecture in England. Like the other Derngate designs, the guest bedroom no longer exists, but it has been reconstructed in the Hunterian Art Gallery, Glasgow. The room is less overpowering than the photograph suggests, since the impact of the stripes is softened by adjacent white walls and mahogany furniture. Nevertheless the owner, W.J. Bassett-Lowke, asked one guest, the Irish dramatist George Bernard Shaw, whether the decor would interfere with his sleep. The sage retorted 'No. I sleep with my eyes shut.'

◁ **Chair** c1916

Ebonized wood

MACKINTOSH'S FURNITURE was always designed for a specific environment, and what appear to be eccentricities in his work often fall away when an individual piece is seen in relation to the overall scheme. This high-backed chair was made for the living room at 78 Derngate, Northampton, where it harmonized with the other elements, notably a very large screen with a similar lattice design; as on comparable features at *The Ingram Street Tea Rooms* (see page 67), some of the squares are filled in and others left open. The lattice features derived in part from Mackintosh's enduring interest in Japanese design, but there is a distinctly art deco feeling to the 'stepped' decorations at the front of the chair and on the top rail of the back. However, the severity of the design is modified by the fact that the back is slightly curved when seen in profile.

▷ **Clock** 1917

Ebonized wood with plastic inlays

MACKINTOSH DESIGNED SEVERAL CLOCKS for W.J. Bassett-Lowke's Northampton house, 78 Derngate. This striking 'domino' clock is not seen in the original photographs of the interior, so it must be a little later than the others; but it was evidently made while the First World War was being fought, since the casing was made by German craftsmen interned on the Isle of Man. At Derngate, Mackintosh made extensive use of black, and also of Erinoid, an early form of plastic. These were to be characteristic of the burgeoning art deco style, along with a stylish geometry, typified by the sets of parallel lines running away from the 'dominoes' and leading the eye, like the clock hands, round the dial. The use of dots instead of numbers is the kind of smart touch that we associate with art deco in, for example, ocean liner interiors and Hollywood movies.

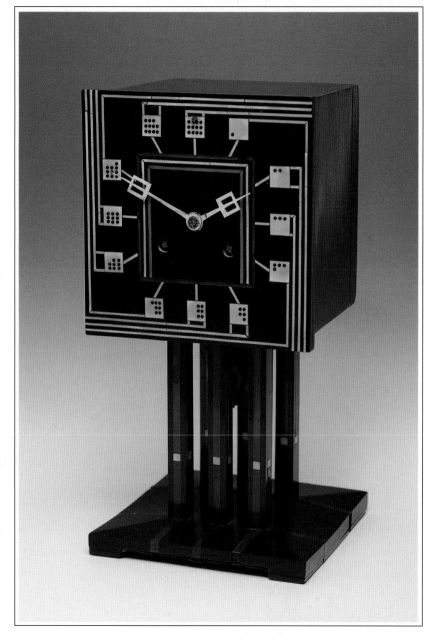

◁ **Rose and Teardrop Design**
1916-23

Despite his innovative work at Derngate (see pages 70-73), Mackintosh had no significant opportunity to exercise his talents for the rest of the war. His prospects improved briefly in 1920, but the more ambitious schemes with which he was involved, including a little theatre in Chelsea, were never realized. However, from about 1916 he and Margaret seem to have made an adequate if uncertain income as freelance textile designers, working for well-known London firms such as Foxton's and Sefton's; in the only year for which records now exist, 1920, Charles and Margaret earned about £200, which in those days was quite a respectable sum. The *Rose and Teardrop Design* shows how skilfully Mackintosh adapted to this new line of work, taking the head of a cabbage rose, which he had formerly shown in isolation on its stalk, and using it as the basis for a dense, strong, repeated pattern.

▷ Design of Blue and Pink Tobacco Flowers 1916-23

This is an original textile design by Mackintosh, carrying his name and the Chelsea address where he and his wife Margaret lived between 1915 and 1923. Mackintosh's designs are rarely easy to date, since most of the records kept by Foxton's and Sefton's have disappeared or were destroyed by enemy bombs during the Second World War. Yet it seems clear that Mackintosh tackled the work with his customary meticulousness. This design is known to have been inspired by the hair of a figure in one of Margaret's decorative panels, *The Opera of the Sea*; but the end result, an intense cluster of floral and geometric motifs, has little in common with her feeling for melancholy fairyland themes. These and other colourful fabric designs by Mackintosh give no hint of the depression and discouragement from which he increasingly suffered as his more ambitious schemes foundered.

▷ **Collioure** c1924

Watercolour

IN 1923 MACKINTOSH gave up the struggle to re-make his career as an architect and interior designer. He and Margaret moved to a part of the South of France, close to the Spanish border, where they could live cheaply and Mackintosh could try to make a new reputation as a watercolour artist. For a time they stayed at Collioure, a seaside village which had been a favourite resort of painters such as Picasso and Matisse some 20 years before; Matisse in particular had made a breakthrough there, painting some masterworks in the blazingly colourful Fauve style. The intense light and brilliant colours of the South encouraged Mackintosh's predilection for hardness and clarity, and nothing could be less like the conventional misty watercolour than this unusual view of Collioure from the sea.

◁ **Le Fort Maillart** 1927

Watercolour

AFTER LEAVING COLLIOURE, the Mackintoshes moved a little way along the coast to Port Vendres. During these years, Mackintosh's most interesting paintings were those in which a feeling for the reality of nature was finely balanced against stark masses and strong patterns. Consequently he found his most rewarding subjects in dense groups of hill houses and the harsh, rocky configuration of the local countryside. He was also fascinated by the old forts in the area, built to defend the border with Spain. These elements come together in *Le Fort Maillart*, whose faceted and layered rocks also have affinities with much avant-garde art of the period. In 1927 Mackintosh developed cancer of the tongue and went to England for treatment. He never returned to France, dying in London on 10 December 1928.

ACKNOWLEDGEMENTS

The publisher would like to thank the following for their kind permission to reproduce the paintings in this book:

Bridgeman Art Library, London/Bridgeman Art Library, London: 20, 21, 24, 62, 63, 65; /**Victoria & Albert Museum, London**: 14, 72; /**Glasgow University Art Gallery**: 16-17, 32-33; /**Glasgow School of Art**: 22, *23*, 25; /**Private Collection**: 35, *68*, 69; /**The Fine Art Society, London**: 37, *50*, 51, 75, 76-77;

Glasgow School of Art: 10, 11, *18*, 19, 31, *46*, 47 *(also used on front cover, back cover detail and half-title page detail)*, *48*, 49, 64, 66

Hunterian Art Gallery: 12, 13, 28, 30, *54*, 55, 58-59, 71

Glasgow University: *26*, 27, 29, 42-43, 56-57, 60-61, 74, 78

Peter Davenport: 38-39, 40-41, *52*, 53

Angelo Hornak: 45

Glasgow Museums: 67

Unattributed: 8, 44

NB: Numbers shown in italics indicate a picture detail.

Every effort has been made to trace the copyright holders and we apologise in advance for any unintentional omissions. We would be pleased to insert the appropriate acknowledgement in any subsequent edition of this publication.